Grammar Practice Workbook

GRADE 1

Printed in the U.S.A.

ISBN 978-0-358-22679-6

1 2 3 4 5 6 7 8 9 10   0928   28 27 26 25 24 23 22 21 20 19

4500768328   A B C D E F G

Grade 1

Contents

Complete Sentences

> A **sentence** is a group of words that tells a complete idea.

▶ **Draw a line under each sentence.**

1. The boy throws a ball.

2. a dog

3. The cat purrs softly.

4. jump

5. Cam and Matt

▶ **Draw lines to make sentences.**

6. Sally   is wearing its collar.

7. The dog   dive into the pool.

8. We   won the game!

9. Our team   draws pictures.

10. The swimmers   eat apples and grapes.

1

Forming Complete Sentences

▶ **Draw a line under each sentence.**

1. The man cleans his car.

   cleans his car.

2. Sleeps well.

   The boy sleeps well.

3. The woman jogs every day.

   The woman

4. He reads books.

   reads books.

5. John and Sarah play tag.

   John and Sarah

6. She paints.

   Paints.

7. We rode our bikes.

   rode our bikes.

8. Manny lost a tooth.

   lost a tooth.

9. Frogs and toads

   Frogs and toads hop.

10. Ellen sold tickets.

    Sold tickets.

▶ **Revisit a piece of your writing. Edit the draft to make sure complete sentences are used correctly.**

Complete and Incomplete Sentences

A **sentence** is a group of words. A sentence tells who or what. It also tells what someone or something does or did.

Sentence	Not a Sentence
All birds have feathers.	have feathers
	all birds

▶ **Circle the two groups of words that are not sentences.**

1. They are smart.

2. are hungry.

3. The door opens.

4. a cup of milk

5. We laugh a lot.

6. Sam will go.

▶ **Add words to make the word groups you circled complete sentences. Write the new sentences.**

7. We are hungry

8. I ee a cup of milk

Review Complete Sentences

A **sentence** tells who or what. It also tells what someone or something does or did.

Sentence	Not a Sentence
Some girls play tag.	Some girls
	play tag.

▶ **Draw a line under each sentence.**

1. We will

2. My mom baked it.

3. He is

4. the cake

5. We enjoyed the party.

6. It started on time.

▶ **Add words to each word group to make a complete sentence.**

7. My favorite treat
is ice cream

8. It is hard
but I dont give up

▶ **Revisit a piece of your writing. Edit the draft to make sure all complete sentences are used correctly.**

Connect to Writing:
Using Complete Sentences

▶ **Read the selection and choose the best answer to each question.**

James wrote the following paragraph about going to a pet shop. Read his paragraph and look for any revisions he should make. Then answer the questions that follow.

(1) We went shopping on Saturday. (2) ~~wanted to shop in the~~ ~~pet store.~~ (3) My sister wanted to shop in the craft store. (4) ~~My father~~ (5) My mother flipped a coin to be fair. (6) I won. (7) ~~to the pet store.~~

1. Which group of words is a complete sentence?

   A. Sentence 1   **B.** Sentence 2

   C. Sentence 4   **D.** Sentence 7

2. Which group of words is NOT a complete sentence?

   A. Sentence 1   **B.** Sentence 3

   C. Sentence 4   **D.** Sentence 6

▶ **Where have you gone shopping? What did you see there? Write two or three complete sentences about it.**

Name _____

Sentence Parts

A **sentence** is a group of words that tells a complete idea. It has two parts. The naming part is called the **subject**. The action part is called the **predicate**.

Subject	Predicate
Jayden	jumps over the curb.
The boy	ran into his house.

▶ **Draw a line under each sentence that has a subject and a predicate.**

1. The spider climbs up the web.

2. My friends

3. The window is broken.

4. A hawk flew over the house.

5. sings songs to the baby

▶ **Revisit a piece of your writing. Edit the draft to make sure all sentence parts are used correctly.**

The Naming Part

A **sentence** is a group of words that tells a complete idea. It has two parts. The **subject** is the naming part. It tells who or what does or did something.

<u>The coach</u> talked to her team.

▶ **Draw a line under the naming part of the sentence.**

1. Kareem grows apples.

2. My dad likes the beach.

3. The roses bloom in June.

4. The rabbit hopped away.

5. Donna sings in the chorus.

6. The cookies are warm.

▶ **Write a naming part from the box to complete each sentence.**

| Hamsters | The roof | Pancakes |

7. ___Hamsters___ run in their cages.

8. ___The roof___ leaks when it rains.

▶ **Revisit a piece of your writing. Edit the draft to make sure all sentence parts are used correctly.**

The Action Part

A **predicate** is the action part of a sentence. A predicate tells what the subject in a sentence does or did.

Jeff <u>laughs at jokes</u>.

▶ **Circle the words to complete each sentence with a predicate, or action part.**

1. Ken _____. (listens in class, in class)

2. Linda _____. (skip home, will skip home)

3. My friend _____. (builds model cars, model cars)

4. Mom _____. (cuts apple slices, apple slices)

5. Pedro _____. (his drum, beats on his drum)

▶ **Revisit a piece of your writing. Edit the draft to make sure all sentence parts are used correctly.**

8

Review Sentence Parts

A **sentence** is a group of words that tells a complete idea. It has two parts. The naming part is called the **subject**. The action part is called the **predicate**.

Naming Part	Action Part
Sharmel	threw the ball.
The cat	climbed up the fence.

▶ **Draw a line under each sentence that has both a naming part and an action part.**

1. in the yard
2. runs fast
3. He sings very well.
4. Cal fixed the leak.
5. helps others

6. Jenna feeds her pet.
7. The dog has fur.
8. skips a lot
9. they are
10. Dina paints the room.

▶ **Revisit a piece of your writing. Edit the draft to make sure all sentence parts are used correctly.**

Connect to Writing: Using Sentence Parts Correctly

▶ **Read the selection and choose the best answer to each question.**

> Donna wrote the following paragraph about her father's tools. Read her paragraph and answer the questions that follow.

(1) My father has new tools. (2) They were a gift. (3) We surprised him! (4) My father likes them a lot. (5) My mother them out. (6) My father let me use them.

1. Which of the sentences has the same subject?
   A. Sentences 1 and 2　　B. Sentences 1 and 4
   C. Sentences 2 and 6　　D. Sentences 3 and 5

2. Choose the correct predicate to make sentence (5) complete.
   A. My mother sleeps them out.
   B. My mother jumped them out.
   C. My mother picked them out.
   D. My mother sings them out.

▶ **Is there a time when you were surprised? Write two or three sentences about it.**

Statements

> A statement begins with a **capital letter** and ends with a **period**.   **The bird builds a nest.**

▶ **Draw a line under each statement.**

1. She likes to dance.

2. twirl and spin

3. You must listen to the beat.

4. It takes plenty of practice.

5. Debbie and Jane

6. We stretch before class.

▶ **Use a word from the box to make each group of words a statement. Make sure you use a capital letter at the beginning of a sentence and a period at the end.**

> shopped   pilots   Malek   sing

7. _____ Malek _____ plays the piano.

8. John and Samantha _____ sing _____.

9. Eleni _____ shopped _____.

10. _____ pilots _____ fly airplanes.

Forming Statements

A statement begins with a **capital letter** and ends
with a **period**.

▶ **Fix the mistakes in these statements. Use
proofreading marks.**

Proofreading Marks	
⊙	add period
≡	capital letter

Example: we dance to the music⊙
         ≡

1. he plays the guitar

2. there is a big mirror

3. she uses the high bar

4. the class is very fun

5. all of the students leave

▶ **Revisit a piece of your writing. Edit the draft to
make sure all statements are used correctly.**

Writing Statements

▶ **Circle the capital letter that begins each statement and the period that ends it.**

1. Jude likes football.

2. He played in the big game.

3. Talia scored six points.

4. Fans cheered for the players.

▶ **Write each statement correctly.**

5. the bleachers are full

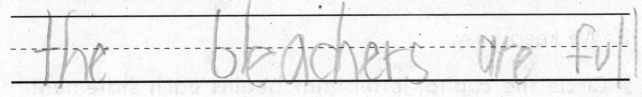

the bleachers are full

6. there is a game next week

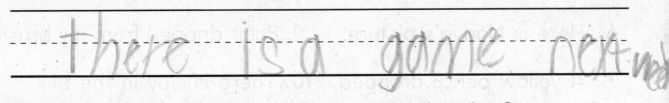

there is a game next week

▶ **Revisit a piece of your writing. Edit the draft to make sure all statements are used correctly.**

Review Statements

A sentence that tells something is called a **statement**.
A statement begins with a capital letter and ends with
a period.

The children make arts and crafts.
Some boys work on puzzles.

▶ **Draw a line under each statement.**

1. This is a fun game.

2. All of the teachers

3. We keep busy.

4. Books are on the shelf.

5. has a puppet

▶ **Circle the capital letter that begins each statement and the period that ends it.**

6. Here is Nadya's picture.

7. A yellow pencil dropped on the floor.

8. Children create art.

9. Paint dripped from my brush.

10. There is clay in the bin.

▶ **Revisit a piece of your writing. Edit the draft to make sure all statements are used correctly.**

Connect to Writing:
Using Statements

▶ **Read the selection and choose the best answer to each question.**

> Mai wrote the following paragraph about going to the pool. Read her paragraph and look for revisions she should make. Then answer the questions that follow.

(1) We live near a pool (2) we like to walk to the pool. (3) Our mother walks with us. (4) I play in the water. (5) my sister likes the slide (6) We always have fun.

1. Which statement is NOT written correctly?
   - **A.** Sentence 3
   - **B.** Sentence 4
   - **C.** Sentence 5
   - **D.** Sentence 6

2. Which statement is written correctly?
   - **A.** Sentence 1
   - **B.** Sentence 2
   - **C.** Sentence 5
   - **D.** Sentence 6

▶ **Where do you like to go in your neighborhood? Write two or three statements about it. Be sure to start your sentences with a capital letter and end them with a period.**

_____

Commands

Commands are simple sentences that tell someone to do something. A command begins with a **capital letter** and ends with a **period**.

▶ **Fix the mistakes in these commands. Use proofreading marks.**

Proofreading Marks	
≡	capital letter
⊙	add period

1. come home

2. bring the book

3. paint the door

4. call me soon

5. find the key

▶ **Revisit a piece of your writing. Edit the draft to make sure all commands are written correctly.**

Commands with That, This, Those

Commands are simple sentences that tell someone to do something. The words **that**, **this**, and **those** are often used in commands.

Walk **this** way.

▶ **Draw a line under each command.**

1. Come (when) I call you.

2. I (will) call you soon.

3. (Run) around the track.

4. She (can) run fast.

▶ **Read each command. Circle the words that, this, and those.**

5. Look (this) way.

6. Watch (those) ducks.

7. Bring (that) box.

8. Open (that) door.

9. Take (those) pens.

10. Ride (this) bike.

▶ **Revisit a piece of your writing. Edit the draft to make sure all commands are written correctly.**

Commands with That, These, Those

> **Commands** are simple sentences that tell someone to do something. The words **that**, **these**, and **those** are often used in commands.
>
> Take **these** papers to school.

▶ **Read each command. Circle the words that, these, and those.**

1. Pack these books.

2. Put those cans in the bin.

3. Play that music quietly.

4. Keep these gloves in the drawer.

5. Ring these bells.

6. Close that window.

7. Catch that ball.

8. Fold those sheets.

9. Buy those apples for lunch.

10. Spell these words.

▶ **Revisit a piece of your writing. Edit the draft to make sure all commands are written correctly.**

Grade 1 • Commands

Printable

Name _____

Name _____

Review Commands

A sentence that tells someone to do something is a command. Commands often use the words **this**, **that**, **these**, and **those**.

Commands	
Fill that cup.	Follow those signs.
Listen to me.	Read these pages.

▶ **Draw a line under each command.**

1. Pick up your socks.

2. Raise your hand.

3. I can smell those flowers.

4. I will call you.

5. Ask your parents.

▶ **Read each command. Circle the words this, that, these, and those.**

6. Take that road.

7. Watch those runners.

8. Knock on that door.

9. Write these names.

10. Jump over this box.

▶ **Revisit a piece of your writing. Edit the draft to make sure all commands are written correctly.**

Connect to Writing: Using Commands

▶ **Read the selection and choose the best answer to each question.**

> Treena wrote this paragraph. Read it and look for changes she should make. Then answer the questions.

(1) I love to jump rope. (2) I will tell you how. (3) find a jump rope (4) Hold one end in each hand. (5) Put your arms at your sides. (6) step the rope over. (7) Swing the rope over your head. (8) Jump over it. (9) Swing it over your head again. (10) Keep going!

1. Which is the best way to rewrite sentence 3?

   A. find a jump rope.   **B.** Find a jump rope

   C. Find a jump rope?   **D.** Find a jump rope.

2. Which of the following could replace sentence 6 and make it better?

   A. Tell you to step over the rope.

   B. Step over the rope.

   C. Stepping over the rope.

   D. Then I will step over the rope.

Subjects and Verbs

Every complete sentence has a **subject** and a **verb**. The subject is the naming part of the sentence. The verb is the action part of the sentence.

subject verb

The horse runs.

▶ **Circle the verb that tells what the subject is doing.**

1. The bird (fly, flies) to the tree.

2. The friends (build, builds) a castle.

3. Kris (talk, talks) to Tim.

4. The girls (play, plays) soccer.

5. The car (stop, stops) at the light.

▶ **Revisit a piece of your writing. Edit the draft to make sure subjects and verbs are used correctly.**

Subject and Verb Agreement

A **verb** has to agree with the **subject** in a sentence.
When a subject names one, add -s to most verbs. When
a subject is more than one, do not add -s to the verb.

The **ball** rolls.   The **balls** roll.

▶ **Choose the correct verb to agree with the underlined subject. Write the verb to finish each sentence.**

1. ~~play~~
   plays

   Many children _____ play _____ by the lake.

2. jump
   ~~jumps~~

   A boy _____ jumps _____ in the water.

3. hit
   ~~hits~~

   The player _____ hits _____ the ball.

4. (rest)
   rests

   Two dogs _____ rest _____ on the grass.

5. (sing)
   sings

   The girls _____ sing _____ a new song.

▶ **Revisit a piece of your writing. Edit the draft to make sure subjects and verbs are used correctly.**

Verbs with -s

Add -s to a verb when it tells about a noun that names one.

Do not add -s to a verb when it tells about a noun that names more than one.

▶ **Fix the mistakes in these sentences. Use proofreading marks.**

Proofreading Marks	
^ add	___ᵍ take out

Examples: Snowflakes ~~falls~~ on the ground.
               fall
               ^

1. Dan get his skates.
   gets

2. Juanita and Carmela plays in the sand.
   play

3. Amir draw a picture.
   draws

4. The dog dig a hole.
   digs

5. Arie and Jo paints the wall.
   Paint

▶ **Revisit a piece of your writing. Edit the draft to make sure subjects and verbs are used correctly.**

Review Subjects and Verbs

In a sentence, the **subject** and the **verb** have to agree. Both must tell about the same number of people or things. Add *-s* to most verbs when they tell about a noun that names one.

Dolphins **swim** in the ocean.   A duck **swims** in a pond.

▶ **Choose the correct verb to finish the sentence.**

1. Stan (look, looks) at the painting.

2. Kareem and Nan (join, joins) the game.

3. Many visitors (come, comes) to the museum.

4. Ricardo (fill, fills) the cup.

5. Seven people (wait, waits) for the bus.

▶ **Revisit a piece of your writing. Edit the draft to make sure subjects and verbs are used correctly.**

Connect to Writing: Using Subjects and Verbs Correctly

▶ **Read the selection and choose the best answer to each question.**

> Antonio wrote the following paragraph about a park. Read his paragraph and look for any revisions he should make. Then answer the questions that follow.

(1) The park is a very busy place. (2) Ducks swim in the pond. (3) A turtle sleeps on a rock. (4) Teams games. (5) I go to the park with Aunt Helen. (6) She take photos. (7) I draw pictures.

1. A word is missing from sentence 4. Which is the best way to fix sentence 4?

   A. Teams make games
   B. Teams makes games.
   C. Teams play games.
   D. Teams plays games.

2. Which change, if any, will improve sentence 6?

   A. Change take to takes.
   B. Change photos to photo.
   C. Change she to he.
   D. No change.

▶ **What is something you like to do? How do you do it? Write two or three sentences about it.**

Questions

> A question is a sentence that asks something.
> A question ends with a **question mark**.
>
> Can you play**?**_

▶ **Underline the sentences that are questions.**

1. What did you see? 5. Can you look up?

2. Is that the sun? 6. I think I will read.

3. Where did Esteban go? 7. They are at the game.

4. How many stamps does Leah have? 8. I like to tell jokes.

▶ **Choose one question from above. Add details and write your new question.**

9. _____

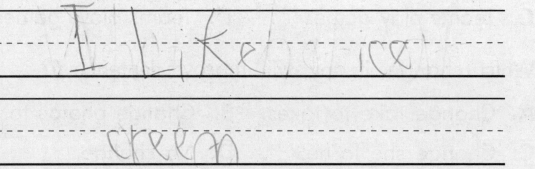

I Like ice

creen

▶ **Revisit a piece of your writing. Edit the draft to make sure questions are used correctly.**

Using Questions

Many questions begin with **what**, **can**, **when**, **where**, **do**, or **are**.

Can you join us?   **Are** you on the team?

▶ Write the correct word from the Word Bank to begin each sentence. Write the correct end mark.

What   Can   When   Where   Do   Are

1. _Where_ can I hang my jacket _?_

2. _Can_ you help me _?_

3. _are_ you busy after school _?_

4. _What_ is for dinner tonight _?_

5. _when_ do you leave for vacation _?_

Writing Questions

A sentence that asks something is called a **question**. A question begins with a capital letter and ends with a **question mark**.

▶ **Fix the mistakes in these sentences. Use proofreading marks.**

Proofreading Marks	
^	add
≡	capitalize

Example: d̲id you water the plants? ^

1. Did you know his name

2. when did they go to the movie?

3. Why do you have your bike.

4. what do cats eat?

5. is it raining.

▶ **Revisit a piece of your writing. Edit the draft to make sure questions are used correctly.**

Review Using Questions

A question always begins with a capital letter and ends
with a question mark. <u>A</u>re you going to the park<u>?</u>

▶ **Write each question correctly.**

1. are you going to the beach

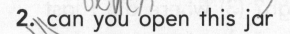
Are you going to the beach

2. can you open this jar

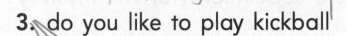
Can you open this jar?

3. do you like to play kickball

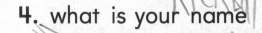
Do you like to play kickball

4. what is your name

What is your name

5. when does school start

When does school start

Name _____

Grammar
1.6.5

Connect to Writing:
Using Questions

▶ **Read the selection and choose the best answer
to each question.**

> Eli wrote the following paragraph about a mystery. Read
> his paragraph and look for any revisions he should
> make. Then answer the questions that follow.

(1) I lost my sock. (2) Where did it go? (3) where did I last
see it (4) I look in the washer. (5) I look in the dryer. (6) The
sock isn't there. (7) Then I have an idea. (8) I look in my
dog's bed. (9) My dog, Pete, is a sock thief! (10) The mystery
is solved.

1. Which is the best way to fix sentence 3?

  A. Where did I last see it   B. Where did I last see it.

  C. where did I last see it?   D. Where did I last see it?

2. Which sentence could you add between sentences 6 and 7
   to improve the paragraph?

  A. Can a sock run away.   B. can a sock run away?

  C. Can a sock run away?   D. Can a sock run away

Grade 1 • Questions

Printable
30
© Houghton Mifflin Harcourt Publishing Company. All rights reserved.

Compound Questions and Statements

A **compound sentence** is made up of two shorter sentences joined by a comma and **and**, **but**, or **or**.

We can swim in the pool, **or** we can go to the lake.

▶ **Underline each compound sentence.**

1. The girls walked or rode the bus to school.

2. Mom drives to work, but Dad takes a train.

3. Is the game today, or is it tomorrow?

4. We have to fold and put away towels.

5. I use the top bunk, and my dog sleeps on the bottom.

6. Sometimes we go bowling, but not today.

▶ **Write a compound sentence by combining the two shorter sentences. Use the joining word shown in ( ).**

7. You have juice. I have milk. **(but)**

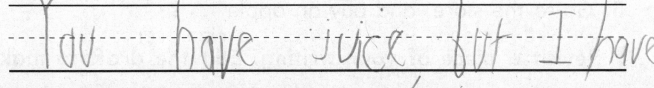

You have juice but I have

8. I can draw. I can paint. **(or)**

_____

- - - - - - - - - - - - - - - - - - - -

_____

Forming Questions and Statements

A **compound sentence** is made up of two simple sentences that are joined by a comma and the word **and**, **but**, or **or**.

Compound questions end with a question mark.

Compound statements and commands end with a period.

Do you want to ski?   Would you rather skate?

Do you want to ski, **or** would you rather skate?

▶ **Circle the correct end mark to finish each compound sentence.**

1. Stay in line, and wait for the bell **(.)** **?**

2. Is your sister here, or is she at home **.** **(?)**

3. Will you watch the movie, or is it too late **.** **(?)**

4. Frogs are smooth, but toads are bumpy. **(.)** **?**

5. Go to the store, and buy an apple **(.)** **?**

▶ **Revisit a piece of your writing. Edit the draft to make sure compound questions and statements are used correctly.**

Writing Compound Questions and Statements

Write a **compound sentence** by combining each pair of shorter sentences. Use a comma and **and**, **but**, or **or** to combine the sentences.

Walk the dog. Feed the cat.
Walk the dog, **and** feed the cat.

▶ **Circle the correct word in ( ) that will combine the shorter sentences into a compound sentence. Choose a period or question mark at the end.**

1. Are you ready (and but or) should I wait . **?**

2. I feel good (and but or) Jorge is sick . **?**

3. The party is Friday (and but or) I am excited . **?**

4. Do you want a ride (and but or) will you walk home . **?**

5. I had a ticket (and but or) I lost it . **?**

▶ **Revisit a piece of your writing. Edit the draft to make sure compound questions and statements are used correctly.**

Review Compound Questions and Statements

Compound sentences and questions are made up of two simple sentences. The two sentences are connected by the word **and**, **but**, or **or**.

▶ **Underline each compound sentence.**

1. What is his name, and how old is he?

2. The work is hard. I need help.

3. I like grapes or peaches.

4. We went to the market, but it was closed.

5. Lupé can help cook, or she can set the table.

6. Feed the fish, and wash the tank.

▶ **Circle the correct word in ( ) that will combine the shorter sentences into a compound sentence. Choose a period or question mark at the end.**

7. The sun is out (and but or) the air is warm . ?

8. Are you coming (and but or) do you want to stay home . ?

Connect to Writing: Compound Questions

▶ **Read the selection and choose the best answer to each question.**

> Oliver wrote the following paragraph. Look for revisions he should make. Then answer the questions.

(1) I like ice skating. (2) My sister does not skate well.
(3) I put my skates on, but my sister stayed on the bench.
(4) I asked, "Do you want help?" (5) I asked, "Do you want to go home?" (6) She let me help her, and she had a great time.

1. How could you combine sentences 1 and 2 to make a compound statement?

   A. I like ice skating, or my sister does not skate well.

   B. I like ice skating, but my sister does not skate well.

2. How could you combine sentences 4 and 5?

   A. I asked, "Do you want help, or do you want to go home?"

   B. I asked, "Do you want help and do you want to go home."

Exclamations

An **exclamation** is a sentence that shows strong feeling. An exclamation begins with a capital letter and ends with an exclamation point.

Meg is the best artist I know!

▶ **Draw a line under each exclamation.**

1. I have good news!

2. Mandy drew a picture of a cat.

3. Karl really likes to paint.

4. Stop right there!

5. Chika has a nice hat.

6. The movie was amazing!

7. Carlos wrote an interesting story.

8. Dad is taking us out for lunch!

9. Donita's team won again!

10. The siren is very loud.

▶ **Revisit a piece of your writing. Edit the draft to make sure exclamations are used correctly.**

Using Exclamations

> An **exclamation** is a sentence that shows strong feeling. An exclamation begins with a capital letter and ends with an exclamation point.

▶ **Write each sentence as an exclamation.**

1. the story was exciting

   _____

   -

   _____

2. please help us

   _____

   -

   _____

3. you did a great job

   _____

   -

   _____

4. i can't wait to get home

   _____

   -

   _____

5. we climbed to the top

   _____

   -

   _____

Name _____

Writing Exclamations

An **exclamation** is a sentence that shows strong feeling. It begins with a capital letter and ends with an exclamation point.

▶ **Write each sentence as an exclamation.**

1. it's finally summer

----

2. that puppy chews everything

----

3. this lemonade is so tasty

----

4. the roof is leaking

----

5. i love to read

Review Exclamations

Use a capital letter and end with an exclamation point.

Statement: Peg writes poems.

Revised: Peg is the best poet!

▶ **Revise each sentence. Make it an exclamation.**

1. Claudio plays soccer.

2. Those peaches taste good.

3. Sheila won a prize.

4. The spider came closer.

5. Do not go so fast.

Connect to Writing: Using Exclamations

▶ **Read the selection and choose the best answer.**

> Carlos wrote a passage about an essay contest. Read his paragraph and look for any revisions he should make. Then answer the questions that follow.

(1) Our school had a writing contest. (2) Everyone had to write an essay. (3) We had to write about something we loved. (4) The winner would get a prize. (5) I really wanted to win. (6) I wrote about my dog, Rascal. (7) Rascal is the best dog ever! (8) On Monday, I found out I won!

1. How could you rewrite sentence 4 to show stronger feeling?

   A. What does the winner get?

   B. The winner would get ten dollars!

2. Which two sentences show the strongest feeling?

   A. Sentences 7 and 8

   B. Sentences 3 and 4

Kinds of Sentences

A **statement** and a **command** end with a period. A **question** ends with a question mark. An **exclamation** ends with an exclamation point.

▶ **Change each sentence to the kind shown in ( ).**

1. Marjan sings a lot. (exclamation)

   _____

   -

   _____

2. Will Jin cook for us? (statement)

   _____

   -

   _____

3. Did you check your spelling? (command)

   _____

   -

   _____

4. Feed the cat. (question)

   _____

   -

   _____

5. Clean your room. (statement)

   _____

   -

   _____

Identifying Kinds of Sentences

A **statement** and a **command** end with a period. A **question** ends with a question mark. An **exclamation** ends with an exclamation point. All sentences begin with a **capital letter**.

▶ **Read each sentence. Circle the correct end mark.**

1. Where is the fork ? ! .

2. I won twenty dollars ? ! .

3. Do you need lunch ? ! .

4. I can't believe it ? ! .

5. Lulu dances in the living room ? ! .

6. Diane is the fastest swimmer ever ? ! .

7. When is your birthday ? ! .

8. Hand the note to Ms. Picolo ? ! .

9. Wendy walked to the store ? ! .

10. It's the best day ever ? ! .

▶ **Revisit a piece of your writing. Edit the draft to make sure all kinds of sentences are used correctly.**

Kinds of Compound Sentences

A **compound sentence** is made up of two simple sentences joined by a comma and **and**, **but**, or **or**. A compound sentence can be a statement, a command, or a question.

▶ **Underline the compound sentences.**

1. Jonah and Ann go to the game.

2. We can make pizza, or we can order it.

3. Is Micah your brother, or is he a friend?

4. Jack or Tom should be at the fair.

▶ **Circle the correct word in ( ) that will combine the shorter sentences into a compound sentence. Choose a period or question mark at the end.**

5. Wash the dog (and but or) feed the fish . ?

6. Do you have a cup (and but or) should I bring you one . ?

7. Jatin likes birds (and but or) they scare me . ?

▶ **Revisit a piece of your writing. Edit the draft to make sure compound sentences are used correctly.**

Review Kinds of Sentences

A **question** ends with a question mark (?). An
exclamation ends with an exclamation point (!).
Statements and **commands** generally end with a period.

▶ **Change each sentence to the kind shown in ( ).**

1. Does Gino like squirrels? (statement)

_____

_____

2. Should I wash my hands? (command)

_____

_____

3. The light is still on. (question)

_____

_____

4. My dog is the best! (statement)

_____

_____

5. I took out the trash. (command)

_____

_____

Connect to Writing:
Using Different Kinds of Sentences

▶ **Read the selection and choose the best answer to each question.**

Regina wrote a passage about her new dog. Read her paragraph and look for any revisions she should make. Then answer the questions that follow.

(1) I wanted a dog. (2) I didn't think I would ever have one. (3) One day, my dad had a surprise for me. (4) We walked to the back yard. (5) There was a dog! (6) I hugged my dad. (7) I named my dog "Max."

1. How could you rewrite sentences 1 and 2 to make a compound sentence?

   A. I wanted a dog, but I didn't think I would ever have one.

   B. I wanted a dog, or I didn't think I would ever have one.

2. What question could be added between sentences 3 and 4?

   A. What did I do?   **B.** What could it be?

Nouns

> Some words name people or animals. Words that name people or animals are called common **nouns**.
>
> Our **principal** is kind.   Do you see the pink **flamingo**?

▶ **Read each sentence. Circle the noun that names a person or an animal.**

1. My cousin will visit.

2. The singer performs.

3. A cat meows.

4. The giraffe has an interesting pattern.

5. The doctor listens to my heart.

6. A pet rabbit would be nice to have.

7. I smell a skunk!

8. The pony trots slowly.

9. My brother and I do chores.

10. The runners are racing.

▶ **Revisit a piece of your writing. Edit the draft to make sure nouns are used correctly.**

Words That Name People

Some words name people. Words that name people are **nouns**.

My **aunt** lives nearby.   The **teacher** is at school.
Some **boys** ate breakfast.

▶ **Read each sentence. Underline the noun that names a person.**

1. The lady is happy.

2. The fireman is my friend.

3. His grandma is visiting.

4. A sailor steered the boat.

5. The pitcher threw the baseball.

6. My brother will be home soon.

7. The dentist checked my teeth.

8. Our neighbor has a new car.

9. I will see my uncle this weekend.

10. Each student will get a folder.

▶ **Revisit a piece of your writing. Edit the draft to make sure nouns that name people are used correctly.**

Words That Name Animals

Some words name animals. Words that name animals are **nouns**.

The **dog** played fetch.   The **elephant** is very smart.

▶ **Read each sentence. Draw a box around the noun that names an animal or animals.**

1. The fish swims in the sea.

2. Does the squirrel like peanuts?

3. The chicken laid more eggs.

4. A whale has many teeth.

5. The pig oinks in his pen.

6. The monkey swings from vine to vine.

7. Can we pet the llama?

8. Hamsters nibble their food.

9. Did you hold the snake?

10. Watch out for alligators!

▶ **Revisit a piece of your writing. Edit the draft to make sure nouns that name animals are used correctly.**

Review Nouns

Some words name people or animals. These words are **nouns**.

My **friend** is nice.   The **kitten** is fluffy.

▶ **Read each sentence. Underline the noun that names a person or an animal.**

1. My sister has braces.

2. The clown is funny.

3. Does the bear really like honey?

4. My dad took me to a movie.

5. A worm wiggled into the ground.

6. A bee stung me!

7. The man got into a taxi.

8. It's time to sheer the woolly sheep.

9. My mom likes to travel.

10. The tiger has long teeth.

▶ **Revisit a piece of your writing. Edit the draft to make sure all nouns are used correctly.**

Connect to Writing: Using Nouns

▶ **Read the selection and choose the best answer to each question.**

Suki wrote the following paragraph about her brother's new job. Read her paragraph and look for any revisions she should make. Then answer the questions that follow.

(1) My brother got a job at a pet shop. (2) Every day, he feeds the. (3) He also helps feed the kittens. (4) His boss, Mr. Jones, let him have a goldfish. (5) He decided to give it to his. (6) They named the goldfish Bubbles.

1. What change should be made to sentence 2?

   A. Every day, he feeds the fluffy.

   B. Every day, he feeds the puppies.

2. Which of the following should replace sentence 5 and make it correct?

   A. He decided to give it to his friend.

   B. He decided to give it to his paper.

Nouns

Words that name people, animals, places, and things are called **nouns**.

The **dancer** jumps.   The **fly** buzzes.

The **rock** falls.   The **street** is busy.

▶ **Read each sentence. Circle the noun that names a person, an animal, a place, or a thing.**

1. The music plays.

2. The sky is clear.

3. My friend loves to dance.

4. Spiders are scary!

5. The hospital was quiet.

6. The restaurant closed.

7. Let's ride in the car.

8. The cat is hungry.

9. The doctor is coming.

10. We are going to the theater.

▶ **Revisit a piece of your writing. Edit the draft to make sure all nouns are used correctly.**

Words That Name Places

> Words that name places are a type of **noun**.
>
> The **circus** was closed.   The **park** is beautiful.

▶ **Read the nouns in the Word Bank. Write a noun from the box to complete each sentence.**

> city   mall   barn   forest   camp

1. There are many trees in the _____

2. Our horses sleep in the _____

3. New York is a busy _____

4. Children take their sleeping bags to _____

5. The _____ has nice stores and a food court.

▶ **Revisit a piece of your writing. Edit the draft to make sure nouns that name places are used correctly.**

Words That Name Things

Words that name things are a type of **noun**.

The **diamond** is pretty.   My **hat** fell off.

Those **cars** are fast.

▶ **Read the nouns in the Word Bank. Write a noun from the box to complete each sentence.**

| hair | tractor | coat | sandwich | sun |

1. Marlon ate a _____

2. I buttoned my _____

3. The _____ is bright.

4. The farmer rides on a _____

5. DeNeal brushes her _____

Review Nouns

> Words that name places and things are called **nouns**.
>
> The **flower** grows.   The **park** is fun.

▶ **Read the nouns in the Word Bank. Write a noun from the box to complete each sentence.**

> library   food   field   bathroom   cup

1. We cooked lots of _____

_____.

2. Kai borrows books from the _____

_____.

3. Clean the shower and sink in your _____

_____.

4. There is hot chocolate in the _____

_____.

5. Cows graze in the _____

_____.

Connect to Writing: Using Nouns

▶ **Read the selection and choose the best answer to each question.**

> Elise wrote the following paragraph. Read her paragraph and look for any revisions she should make. Then answer the questions that follow.

(1) I just went to an amusement park called Fun Land! (2) My ticket was good for a whole day. (3) Was amazing. (4) The roller coasters were so fast! (5) The carousel was slow, but I liked it. (6) Afterwards, I rode a to get home. (7) The park was much more exciting!

1. What should replace sentence 3 to make it correct?

   A. Really amazing park!   **B.** Fun Land was really!

   C. The park was amazing!   **D.** Make no change.

2. Which of the following should replace sentence 6 to make it correct?

   A. Afterwards, I rode a bus to get home.

   B. Afterwards, to get I rode home.

   C. After Fun Land, rode to get home.

   D. Afterwards, I rode a home.

Singular and Plural Nouns

Some **nouns** name **one**. Some nouns name **more than one**. An -s ending means more than one. Some nouns change their spelling to name more than one.

I read three ~~book.~~ ^{books} Two ~~man~~ ^{men} talk.

▶ **Read each sentence. Use proofreading marks to fix the mistakes.**

1. One ducks swims.

2. All of the elephant eat.

3. Three woman sing.

4. I see two tent.

5. A big trucks drove by our house.

Proofreading Marks	
^	add
———ℓ	take out

▶ **Revisit a piece of your writing. Edit the draft to make sure all singular and plural nouns are used correctly.**

One and More Than One

> **Nouns** can name **one** or **more than one**.

▶ **Read each pair of nouns. Circle the plural noun.
Then write the noun you circled.**

1. bird   birds   _____

2. wishes   wish   _____

3. pencil   pencils   _____

4. kites   kite   _____

5. cakes   cake   _____

▶ **Revisit a piece of your writing. Edit the draft to
make sure all singular and plural nouns are used
correctly.**

Name _____

Special Plural Nouns

Some **nouns** that name **more than one** are spelled differently. They do not add **-s** or **-es**.

▶ **Circle the correct noun to complete each sentence.**

1. The (goose, geese) honks.

2. Five (goose, geese) crossed the road.

3. Three (man, men) pushed the truck.

4. That (man, men) is Gia's dad.

5. A (child, children) splashed in the pool.

6. All of the (child, children) listened to a story.

7. Many (woman, women) went outside.

8. A nice (woman, women) answered the door.

9. One small (mouse, mice) scurried away.

10. Some (mouse, mice) live in this barn.

▶ **Revisit a piece of your writing. Edit the draft to make sure all singular and plural nouns are used correctly.**

Review Singular and Plural Nouns

Some nouns name **one**. Some nouns name **more than one** by adding **-s**.

One <u>cat</u> purrs.   Two <u>cats</u> sleep.

Some nouns change spelling to mean more than one.

One <u>man</u> walks.   Two <u>men</u> run.

▶ **Circle the correct noun to complete each sentence. Then write the noun you circled.**

1. Three (hat, hats) are on sale. _____

2. Four (man, men) dance. _____

3. One (egg, eggs) fries in the pan. _____

4. Two (bear, bears) play. _____

5. Three (child, children) got on the bus. _____

Connect to Writing: Using Singular and Plural Nouns

▶ **Read the selection and choose the best answer to each question.**

> Luis wrote the following paragraph about a day in the city. Read his paragraph and look for any revisions he should make. Then answer the questions that follow.

(1) Last week, my friend and I went to the city. (2) We rode in a car to get there. (3) There were many man wearing suits. (4) We went to three restaurants. (5) One woman told us about the city. (6) She said some of the buildings were taller than any others on Earth. (7) We looked at them and fed two bird. (8) What a fun time!

1. What change should be made to sentence 3?

    A. Replace man with men.   **B.** Replace man with mans.

    C. Replace man with mens. **D.** Make no change.

2. Which of the following should replace sentence 7 to make it correct?

    A. We looked at them and feeds two bird.

    B. We looked at them and fed two birds.

Grade 1 • Singular and Plural Nouns

Proper Nouns and Capitalization

A common noun names a person, animal, place, or thing. A **proper noun** always begins with a capital letter.

proper noun   common noun

Sammy is my favorite **cat**.

▶ **Circle the proper noun in each sentence.**

1. Julio has a small dog.

2. My best friend is Stella.

3. Our school is on Main Street.

4. I checked out a book from Hanford Library.

5. My father is from Dallas.

6. I helped Ariel find her lunch box.

7. Our friends are moving to Oklahoma.

8. Woodland Zoo has lions, tigers, and bears.

9. I ate Puffy Pops cereal this morning.

10. Have you been to Yellowstone National Park?

▶ **Revisit a piece of your writing. Edit the draft to make sure all proper nouns are used correctly.**

Names for People, Animals, Places, and Things

> A **proper noun** names a special person, animal, place, or thing and begins with a capital letter.

▶ **Circle each proper noun that names a special person or animal.**

1. Did you help Kim make dinner?

2. It is time for Stanley to go to bed.

3. Miley's fish, Bubbles, is blue and yellow.

4. There was a television show about a dog named Lassie.

5. Please give Asha this note.

▶ **Circle each proper noun that names a special place or thing.**

6. The new school is on Tanner Drive.

7. The Smith Museum has beautiful art.

8. Our favorite juice is Goodness Grapes.

9. There is a prince in England.

10. Will you ride the Super Slide at the fair?

Titles for People

A **title** may be used before a person's name and begins with a capital letter. Some titles end with a period.

▶ **Write the titles and names correctly.**

1. mrs Scott _____

2. mr Garcia _____

3. dr hill _____

▶ **Draw a line under each title. Then write the title and name correctly.**

4. miss Fisher plays the piano. _____

5. Where does dr Diaz live? _____

▶ **Revisit a piece of your writing. Edit the draft to make sure all proper nouns and titles are used correctly.**

Review Proper Nouns and Capitalization

A **proper noun** names a special person, animal, place or thing and begins with a capital letter.

When a **title** is used before a name, it begins with a capital letter and ends with a period.

▶ **Write each proper noun and title correctly. Add a period if needed.**

1. We met mrs Bell. _____

2. Her dog is named snuffles. _____

3. They went on vacation to florida. _____

4. We drove down elm street. _____

5. He met roberto at the movies. _____

Connect to Writing: Using Proper Nouns

▶ **Read the selection and choose the best answer to each question.**

Hugo wrote the following paragraph about his first day at a new school. Read his paragraph and look for any revisions he should make. Then answer the questions that follow.

(1) I was so scared on my first day of school. (2) My new teacher, mrs Ramirez, put me next to a boy named Ibraham. (3) Mrs. Ramirez put me next to ibraham because we like a lot of the same things. (4) We played soccer together at recess. (5) Then, we read a Dr. Seuss book together. (6) Now, Ibraham is my best friend.

1. What change should be made to sentence 2?

   A. Change mrs to mr.   **B.** Change Ramirez to ramirez.

   C. Change mrs to Mrs.   **D.** Make no change.

2. What change should be made to sentence 3?

   A. Change Mrs. to mrs.   **B.** Change ibraham to Ibraham.

   C. Change Mrs. to mr.   **D.** Change ibraham to hugo.

Names of Months, Days, and Holidays

> The names of **months** of the year, **days** of the
> week, and **holidays** are nouns that name special
> things. They begin with a capital letter.
>
> **Thanksgiving** is celebrated on the fourth **Thursday**
> of **November**.

▶ **Circle the month, day, or holiday in each sentence.**

1. I made my dad a card for Father's Day.

2. Fernanda's birthday is in July.

3. The first day of school is in August.

4. I go to the park every Saturday.

5. We celebrate with friends on New Year's Day.

6. On Monday, the class will take a field trip.

7. We honor soldiers on Veterans Day.

8. The birthstone for June is a pearl.

9. Some people celebrate Arbor Day by planting a tree.

10. Fall begins in September.

Capitalizing Months, Days, and Holidays

> The names of **months** of the year, **days** of the week, and **holidays** always begin with a capital letter.

▶ **Circle the month, day, or holiday in each sentence. Write it correctly on the line.**

1. We had a picnic on labor day. _____

2. My piano lesson is wednesday. _____

3. Spring begins in march. _____

▶ **Draw a line under the correct sentence in each pair.**

4. We got cards on valentine's day.
   We got cards on Valentine's Day.

5. My aunt visited us on Sunday.
   My aunt visited us on sunday.

Commas in Dates, Names, and Nouns

When you write a **date**, put a comma between the number of the day and the year.

The names of **months**, **days**, and **holidays** always begin with a capital letter.

The first **Independence Day** was celebrated on **July** 4, 1777.

▶ **Circle the comma in each date.**

1. George Washington was born on February 22, 1732.

2. Bobbi Gibb ran the Boston Marathon on April 19, 1966.

3. The first moon landing was July 20, 1969.

▶ **Write each date correctly.**

4. march 15 1973 _____

_____

5. january 1 2000 _____

_____

6. april 22 2004 _____

_____

Review Names of Months, Days, and Holidays

The names of **months** in a year, **days** of the week, and **holidays** begin with a capital letter.

Memorial Day is always on a **Monday**.

When you write a **date**, use a comma between the day and the year.

February 3, 1995

▶ **Circle each day or date that is written correctly. Draw a line through any day or date that has errors.**

1. memorial day

2. Valentine's Day

3. january 11, 2011

4. march 27, 2015

5. Presidents' Day

6. August 2, 2010

7. thursday

8. Labor Day

9. Friday

10. Wednesday, May 3 2018

▶ **Revisit a piece of your writing. Edit the draft to make sure the names of months, days, and holidays are used correctly and that commas are used correctly in dates.**

Connect to Writing: Using Names of Months, Days, and Holidays

▶ **Read the selection and choose the best answer to each question.**

Nala wrote the following paragraph about a special birthday and holiday. Read her paragraph and look for any revisions she should make. Then answer the questions that follow.

(1) My little sister was born on july 4 2011. (2) It was independence day, so our dad took us to a big parade. (3) We heard booming drums and saw a marching band. (4) My little brother thought the parade was for our new sister. (5) He said he wanted a parade for his birthday, too.

1. What change should be made to sentence 1?

   A. Change july 4 2011 to July, 4, 2011.

   B. Change july 4 2011 to July 4, 2011.

2. What change should be made to sentence 2?

   A. Change independence day to Independence day.

   B. Change independence day to Independence Day.

Subject Pronouns

A **pronoun** can take the place of a noun.

Jana likes popcorn.   **She** likes popcorn.

She takes the place of **Jana**.

▶ **Circle the pronoun in each sentence.**

1. We play soccer at recess.

2. It seems very late.

▶ **Write a pronoun to take the place of the underlined word or words.**

3. <u>Clara</u> loves to dance. _____

_____

4. <u>Dad</u> helped cook dinner. _____

_____

5. <u>Jonah and Kevin</u> walk to school. _____

_____

Pronouns That Name One

A **pronoun** takes the place of a noun. The pronouns **he**, **she**, and **it** name one.

▶ **Circle the pronoun that can take the place of the underlined word or words.**

1. <u>Grandpa</u> built a birdhouse.   He   She   They

2. <u>The birdhouse</u> is made of wood.   We   She   It

3. <u>Anna</u> helped Grandpa paint the birdhouse.   He   She   We

▶ **Write He, She, or It to take the place of the underlined word or words.**

4. <u>Juana</u> sees a nest. _____

_____

5. <u>The nest</u> has eggs. _____

_____

▶ **Revisit a piece of your writing. Edit the draft to make sure subject pronouns are used correctly.**

Pronouns That Name More Than One

> A **pronoun** takes the place of a noun. The pronouns **we** and **they** name **more than one**.

▶ **Circle the pronoun that can take the place of each underlined subject.**

1. The boys were in a play.   We   They

2. Mom and I watched the play.   We   They

3. Marco and Ryan are good actors.   We   They

▶ **Write We or They to take the place of each underlined subject.**

4. Dad and I walk to the store. _____

5. Pedro and Kristen want some bananas. _____

▶ **Revisit a piece of your writing. Edit the draft to make sure subject pronouns are used correctly.**

Review Subject Pronouns

Words that can take the place of nouns are called **pronouns**. The pronouns **he**, **she**, and **it** name **one**. The pronouns **we** and **they** name **more than one**.

▶ **Write the pronoun that can take the place of each word or words. Choose from the pronouns in the box.**

he	she	it	we	they

1. Aunt Carol _____

_____

2. Ben _____

_____

3. the boys and girls _____

_____

4. my sister and I _____

_____

5. the glass _____

_____

Connect to Writing: Using Subject Pronouns

▶ **Read the selection and choose the best answer to each question.**

> Mariel wrote the following paragraph about her trip to Florida. Read her paragraph and look for places to use pronouns. Then answer the questions that follow.

(1) Last summer my family went to Florida. (2) <u>My parents and I</u> saw dolphins. (3) The best part of our trip was going to Kennedy Space Center. (4) I got to meet some astronauts! (5) <u>The astronauts</u> showed us a real rocket. (6) Maybe one day I'll go to space.

1. Which pronoun could replace the underlined words in sentence 2?

   A. He   **B.** They

   C. It   **D.** We

2. Which pronoun could replace the underlined words in sentence 5?

   A. She   **B.** They

   C. We   **D.** It

Introduce the Pronouns I and Me

> When you talk about yourself as the subject of a sentence, use the **pronoun I**. When you talk about yourself as part of the predicate, use the pronoun **me**.
>
> **I** have the book.   Sunil gave the book to **me**.

▶ **Choose the correct pronoun to complete each sentence.**

1. _____ am happy.   I   me

   _____

2. Mom took _____ to the park.   I   me

   _____

3. John made cookies for _____ I   me

   _____ .

4. _____ can tie my shoes.   I   me

   _____

5. _____ got a new kitten.   I   me

   _____

▶ **Revisit a piece of your writing. Edit the draft to make sure the pronouns *I* and *me* are used correctly.**

Naming Yourself Last

Name yourself last when you talk about yourself and others.

Use the **pronoun I** in the subject of a sentence. Use the objective case pronoun **me** in the predicate.

Correct	Not Correct
Diana and I walk to school.	**I and Diana** walk to school.
They played with **Tomás and me**.	They played with **me and Tomás**.

▶ **Circle the correct words to complete each sentence.**

1. (Han and I, Han and me) see the birds.

2. Dad took (Tia and I, Tia and me) to the movies.

3. (Amy and I, Amy and me) went to the store.

4. (I and my friends, My friends and I) made a fort.

5. My sister reads to (me and Peter, Peter and me).

▶ **Revisit a piece of your writing. Edit the draft to make sure the pronouns I and me are used correctly and I is capitalized.**

Using the Pronouns I, Me, Them, and They

Use the **pronouns I** and **they** in the subject of a sentence. Use the objective case pronouns **me** and **them** in the predicate.

<u>I</u> go to school.   Juan goes to school with <u>me</u>.
They go to school.   Sara goes to school with **them**.

▶ **Circle the correct pronoun to complete each sentence.**

1. Yoshi and (I, me) visited the farm.

2. Mom walked to bus stop with (I, me).

3. My sister went to the zoo with (they, them).

4. (They, Them) and Nayani had a sleepover.

5. Papa handed baskets to Cleo and (I, me).

▶ **Revisit a piece of your writing. Edit the draft to make sure the pronouns I, me, them, and they are used correctly.**

Review the Pronouns *I* and *Me*

Use **I** in the subject of a sentence and **me** in the predicate.

Name yourself last when you talk about yourself and others.

Use **they** in the subject of a sentence and **them** in the predicate.

▶ **Choose the correct pronoun to complete each sentence.**

1. _____ go to the art store. I Me Them

2. He likes to play with _____. I they them

3. Meg gave the hat to _____. I me they

4. _____ made a cake. Me They Them

5. The teacher read to Sierra and _____. I me they

▶ **Revisit a piece of your writing. Edit the draft to make sure the pronouns I, me, them, and they are used correctly.**

Name _____

Connect to Writing: Using the Pronouns *I* and *Me*

▶ **Read the selection and choose the best answer to each question.**

> Alexa wrote the following paragraph. Read her paragraph and look for any revisions she should make. Then answer the questions that follow.

(1) Do you like apples? (2) I and my family love them. (3) We go to pick apples every year. (4) Then my mom and dad cook the apples. (5) Them make applesauce, pies, and cakes. (6) I love apples!

1. What change should be made to sentence 2?

   A. Change I and my family to My family and me.

   B. Change I and my family to My family and I.

2. What change should be made to sentence 5?

   A. Change Them to They.

   B. Change Them to I and them.

Possessive Pronouns

A **possessive noun** and a **possessive pronoun** shows that somebody owns something.

Some possessive pronouns are **my**, **your**, **his**, **her**, and **their**. Possessive nouns use an **apostrophe** and the letter **-s**.

There is milk in <u>**your**</u> cup. (The cup belongs to you.)
<u>**Malik's**</u> ball was under the table. (The ball belongs to Malik.)

▶ **Circle the possessive noun or pronoun in each sentence.**

1. Zane's new shirt is yellow.

2. Marissa borrowed my book.

3. Your pencil is on the desk.

4. Is that her puzzle?

5. That is Mr. Clark's cat.

▶ **Revisit a piece of your writing. Edit the draft to make sure possessive pronouns are used correctly.**

Using My, Your, His, and Her

> The **possessive pronouns my**, **your**, **his**, and **her** show that a person or animal has or owns something. These pronouns come before a noun.
>
> Carol put on **her** <u>coat</u>.　　Will you hold **my** <u>hand</u>?

▶ **Write the correct pronoun to complete each sentence.**

1. I like _____ shoes.　you　your

2. The cat chases _____ tail.　hers　her

3. Sam gives _____ friend a present.　his　him

4. Bring _____ pillow and blanket.　your　you

5. We can play at _____ house.　me　my

▶ **Revisit a piece of your writing. Edit the draft to make sure possessive pronouns are used correctly.**

Using Mine, Yours, His, Hers, Their, and Theirs

Possessive pronouns show that someone owns something. The pronouns **mine**, **yours**, **his**, **hers**, and **theirs** come after a noun and often appear at the end of a sentence.

The red **hat** is **mine**.

The possessive pronoun **their** comes before a noun.

Their house is on the next street.

▶ **Circle the correct pronoun to complete each sentence.**

1. That telescope is _____. theirs their

2. That thermos is _____. hers her

3. This is _____ list of chores. your yours

4. That fluffy puppy is _____. my mine

5. Let's go to _____ house. theirs their

▶ **Revisit a piece of your writing. Edit the draft to make sure possessive pronouns are used correctly.**

Review Possessive Pronouns

Possessive nouns and **pronouns** show that something belongs to someone.

The pronouns **my**, **your**, **his**, **her**, and **their** come before a noun.

The pronouns **mine**, **yours**, **his**, **hers**, and **theirs** come at the end of a sentence.

An **apostprophe** and the **-s** are added to nouns.

▶ **Circle the correct possessive noun or pronoun to complete each sentence.**

1. That is (my, mine) crayon. The crayon is mine.

2. (Theirs, Their) house is green. The green house is theirs.

3. Susan had a cookie. Who ate (Susan's, hers) cookie?

4. Did you ride your bike? The bike is (your, yours).

5. Marcy's hat has stripes. The striped hat is (hers, her).

▶ **Revisit a piece of your writing. Edit the draft to make sure possessive pronouns are used correctly.**

Connect to Writing: Using Possessive Pronouns

▶ **Read the selection and choose the best answer to each question.**

> Luka wrote the following paragraph about a jump rope he found. Read his paragraph and look for any revisions he should make. Then answer the questions that follow.

(1) I found a jump rope at the park. (2) My friend Mikayla said it might be her. (3) The jump rope was blue and green. (4) My other friends, Owen and Rose, said it might be theys. (5) We decided to share the jump rope. (6) We had a fun time playing together!

1. What change should be made to sentence 2?

   A. Change her to hers.   **B.** Change her to my.

   C. Change Mikayla to her.   **D.** Change her to their.

2. What change should be made to sentence 4?

   A. Change theys to our.   **B.** Change theys to their.

   C. Change theys to theirs.   **D.** Change theys to her.

Indefinite Pronouns

> **Indefinite pronouns** are special **pronouns** that stand for people or things that are not named.
>
> Examples of indefinite pronouns include **anyone**, **anything**, **everything**, **someone**, **something**, **nobody**, and **everyone**.

▶ **Circle the correct indefinite pronoun to complete each sentence.**

1. (Everyone, Nobody) is in the empty classroom.

2. Vince asked if (anyone, anything) needs a partner.

3. LaTonya has (something, anything) to tell us.

4. (Anyone, Everyone) had fun at the party.

5. Is there (everything, anything) you need from the store?

▶ **Revisit a piece of your writing. Edit the draft to make sure indefinite pronouns are used correctly.**

Grade 1 · Indefinite Pronouns

Printable
86

Indefinite Pronouns for Nouns Not Named

> **Indefinite pronouns** are special **pronouns** that stand for people or things that are not named.

▶ **Write an indefinite pronoun from the Word Bank to complete each sentence.**

> nothing   anybody   nobody   anything

1. You can learn _____ at the library.

2. _____ should ever swim alone.

▶ **Draw a line under the indefinite pronoun in each sentence.**

3. He knows everything about plants.

4. Someone made a blueberry pie.

5. Would anyone like a banana?

▶ **Revisit a piece of your writing. Edit the draft to make sure indefinite pronouns are used correctly.**

Using Indefinite Pronouns

Indefinite pronouns stand for people or things
that are not named.

▶ Write an indefinite pronoun from the Word Bank to
complete each sentence. There may be more than one
right answer.

anyone   someone   everyone
something   everybody   everything

1. We met _____ on the playground.

2. Did you bring _____ to eat?

3. Can _____ hear me?

4. Marlon put _____ away.

5. _____ likes pizza.

Review Indefinite Pronouns

Indefinite pronouns stand for people or things that are not named. They do not stand for exact or definite persons or things.

Use a singular verb form with an indefinite pronoun.

▶ **Write an indefinite pronoun from the Word Bank to complete each sentence. There may be more than one right answer.**

> anybody   everybody   somebody

1. _____ is working in the school garden.

2. Did _____ bring a shovel?

▶ **Draw a line under the indefinite pronoun in each sentence.**

3. Keiko asked to borrow a hat from someone.

4. I do not want anybody to step on the plants.

5. Ms. Welsh said everything went as planned.

Connect to Writing: Using Indefinite Pronouns

▶ **Read the selection and choose the best answer to each question.**

Eric wrote the following paragraph. Read his paragraph and look for any revisions he should make. Then answer the questions that follow.

(1) One morning we found a big mess in the kitchen. (2) There was nothing sticky all over the floor. (3) My mom asked if anybody knew who made the mess. (4) Everyone said they did not know. (5) Then, something looked at the dog. (6) She had something sticky in her fur. (7) Now we knew who made the mess.

1. What change should be made to sentence 2?

   A. Change nothing to something.

   B. Change nothing to somebody.

2. What change should be made to sentence 5?

   A. Change something to everyone.

   B. Change something to nobody.

Action Verbs

> **Action verbs** tell what people, animals, and things do.

▶ **Read the verbs in the Word Bank. Write a verb to finish each sentence.**

> run   swim   drink   eat   paint

1. I _____ orange juice with my breakfast.

   _____

2. The racers _____ around a track.

   _____

3. We _____ lunch in the cafeteria.

   _____

4. Children _____ with watercolors in art class.

   _____

5. Dolphins _____ in the ocean.

   _____

▶ **Revisit a piece of your writing. Edit the draft to make sure action verbs are used correctly.**

Action Words in the Present

Action verbs tell what people, animals, and things do.

▶ Read the verbs in the Word Bank. Write a verb to finish each sentence.

dig   dance   climbs   hears   marches

1. Simon _____ the alarm beeping.

2. We _____ holes in the sand with our shovel.

3. The band _____ onto the field.

4. Frances _____ to the top of the wall.

5. Guests _____ with the bride and groom.

▶ Revisit a piece of your writing. Edit the draft to make sure action verbs are used correctly.

Using Action Words

Words that name actions are called **verbs**. Verbs tell what people, animals, and things do.

▶ **Circle the verb that belongs in each sentence.**

1. Jill _____ the baseball with a bat. hits fits

2. Airplanes _____ down the runway. zoom take

3. Ben and Lee _____ a dollar on the sidewalk.
   find hop

4. Tigers _____ fiercely. roar row

5. Ella and Kim _____ their favorite song. grow sing

▶ **Revisit a piece of your writing. Edit the draft to make sure action verbs are used correctly.**

Review Action Verbs

Some words tell what people, animals, and things do.
Words that name actions are called **verbs**.
We **jump** on the trampoline.   Sam **dances** to the music.

▶ **Underline the verb in each sentence.**

1. Jan cheers for her teammates.

2. Tina and Bill scrub the floor.

3. We fix the fence.

4. Hana and Tim look at the stars.

5. Kylie shares her toys.

▶ **Revisit a piece of your writing. Edit the draft to make sure action verbs are used correctly.**

Connect to Writing: Using Action Verbs

▶ **Read the selection and choose the best answer to each question.**

> Nina wrote the following paragraph about visiting a garden. Read her paragraph and look for any revisions she should make. Then answer the questions that follow.

(1) It is Saturday. (2) We smile to the garden. (3) Jen and Rob pick berries. (4) I pick flowers. (5) We feed the birds. (6) We sing the plants. (7) We love to visit the garden!

1. What verb could you use to fix sentence 2?

   A. Change smile to walk.   **B.** Change smile to found.

   C. Change smile to nicely.   **D.** Change smile to press.

2. What verb could you use to fix sentence 6?

   A. Change sing to flower.   **B.** Change sing to water.

   C. Change sing to light.   **D.** Change sing to play.

▶ **What do you like to do on a Saturday? Write two or three sentences about it.**

Verbs and Time

> Some **verbs** tell what is happening now. Some verbs tell what happened in the past.
>
> Add **-ed** to most verbs to tell about the past.

▶ **Fix the mistakes in these sentences. Use proofreading marks.**

                              watched
Example: Many people ~~watch~~ the race last night.
                              ^

1. The friends played cards now.

2. Jim and Shira talk yesterday.

3. Last night the cat visits the dog.

4. We race yesterday.

5. The students finish homework last night.

Proofreading Marks	
^	add
‿ꝰ	take out

▶ **Revisit a piece of your writing. Edit the draft to make sure verb tenses are used correctly.**

Verbs with -ed

> Some **verbs** tell what happened in the past. Add **-ed** to most verbs to tell about the past.

▶ **Circle the verbs that tell about the past. Write those verbs.**

1. Sadie _____ at home. stay stayed

_____

2. Alejandro _____ the coins in his bank.

_____

count counted

3. We _____ the train. miss missed

_____

4. The game _____ at 2 o'clock. starts started

_____

5. Ariel _____ at her baby pictures.

_____

looks looked

▶ **Revisit a piece of your writing. Edit the draft to make sure verb tenses are used correctly.**

Present and Past Time

Some **verbs** tell what is happening now. Some verbs tell what happened in the past. Add **-ed** to most verbs to tell about the past.

Words such as **now**, **yesterday**, and **last night** can help tell when an action takes place.

▶ **Circle the correct verb to show present or past time. Write the verb on the line.**

1. Meg _____ her watch every ten minutes. (present time) checks checked

2. Today we _____ the towels. (present time) wash washed

3. Yesterday Ronaldo _____ his dad make lunch. (past time) help helped

4. Now Johan and Katya _____ the gifts. (present time) wrap wrapped

5. Colby _____ us yesterday. (past time) visit visited

▶ **Revisit a piece of your writing. Edit the draft to make sure verb tenses are used correctly.**

Review Verbs in Time

> Some **verbs** tell what is happening now. Some verbs tell what happened in the past. Add **-ed** to most verbs to tell about the past.

▶ **Circle the verb in each sentence. Then write the verb so it tells about the past.**

1. She rocks the baby to sleep. _____

2. Students listen carefully to the teacher. _____

3. Tarique scoops ice cream. _____

4. Jessie and Lola learn to knit. _____

5. The dogs bark at the doorbell. _____

▶ **Revisit a piece of your writing. Edit the draft to make sure all verb tenses are used correctly.**

Connect to Writing: Using Present- and Past-Tense Verbs

▶ **Read the selection and choose the best answer to each question.**

> Victor wrote the following paragraph about going camping. Read his paragraph and look for revisions he should make. Then answer the questions that follow.

(1) My family went camping. (2) We hike up a mountain. (3) We toasted marshmallows in the campfire. (4) We looked at the night sky. (5) We counted the stars. (6) There were a lot of stars! (7) I hope to go camping again soon!

1. Which sentence is NOT written correctly?

   A. Sentence 2   **B.** Sentence 4

   C. Sentence 5   **D.** Sentence 7

2. Which sentence correctly uses a present-tense verb?

   A. We hiking up a mountain.

   B. We looked at the night sky.

   C. We counted the stars.

   D. I hope to go camping again soon!

The Verb Be

The verbs **is** and **are** tell what is happening now. The verbs **was** and **were** tell what happened in the past. Use **is** or **was** with a noun that names one.

▶ **Fix the mistakes in these sentences. Use proofreading marks.**

were
Cats ~~was~~ once kittens.　A kitten ~~are~~ small.
　　　^　　　　　　　　　　　　is
　　　　　　　　　　　　　　　　　^

1. Dogs is smart.

2. The buildings is tall.

3. The flower were blooming last night.

4. The truck are big.

5. My cousins was riding a pony yesterday.

▶ **Revisit a piece of your writing. Edit the draft to make sure the verb be is used correctly.**

Using Is and Are

> The verbs **is** and **are** tell what is happening now.
> Use **is** with a noun that names one. Use **are** with a
> noun that names more than one.

▶ **Circle is or are for each sentence. Then write the
verb to complete the sentence.**

1. Our house _____ blue.   is   are

   _____

2. The boxes _____ heavy.   is   are

   _____

3. Claudio _____ late.   is   are

   _____

4. Snowflakes _____ pretty.   is   are

   _____

5. Maya _____ six years old.   is   are

   _____

▶ **Revisit a piece of your writing. Edit the draft to
make sure the verb be is used correctly.**

Using Was and Were

> The verbs **was** and **were** tell what happened in the past. Use **was** with a noun that names one. Use **were** with a noun that names more than one.

▶ **Circle was or were for each sentence. Then write the verb to complete the sentence.**

1. The clouds _____ puffy. was   were

   _____

2. A frog _____ in the water. was   were

   _____

3. The goats _____ very friendly. was   were

   _____

4. We _____ tired and hungry. was   were

   _____

5. Talia _____ first in line. was   were

   _____

▶ **Revisit a piece of your writing. Edit the draft to make sure the verb be is used correctly.**

Review the Verb Be

> The verbs **is** and **are** tell what is happening now. Use **is** with a noun that names one.
>
> The verbs **was** and **were** tell what happened in the past. Use **was** with a noun that names one.

▶ **Write is or are to complete each sentence.**

1. Alice _____ at school.

2. My parents _____ good cooks.

▶ **Write was or were to complete each sentence.**

3. All of the puppies _____ asleep.

4. The store _____ busy.

5. The students _____ excited.

Connect to Writing: Using the Verb Be

▶ **Read the selection and choose the best answer to each question.**

> Kaya wrote the following paragraph about her pets. Read her paragraph and look for revisions she should make. Then answer the questions that follow.

(1) I have a dog. (2) Her name is Bella. (3) She is black with white patches. (4) She is friendly. (5) I also have two cats. (6) They was scared of Bella. (7) Now they is best friends! (8) I love all my pets.

1. Which sentence uses the wrong verb?

   A. Sentence 2   **B.** Sentence 3

   C. Sentence 6   **D.** Sentence 8

2. Which sentence should replace sentence 7?

   A. Now he is best friends!   **B.** Now they are best friends!

   C. Now they was best friends!   **D.** Now they were best friends!

▶ **Do you like animals? Write a few sentences about your favorite animal.**

_____

Future Tense

You can write sentences that tell what may happen in the future. Use **will** or **is going to** to write sentences about the future.

Marisol **will** sing.   Marisol **is going** to sing.

▶ **Rewrite each sentence to tell about the future.**

1. Jacob jumps high.

_____

- -

_____

2. Rita went to the movies.

_____

- -

_____

▶ **Circle the sentences below that tell about the future.**

3. Dana will ride her bike.

4. Sage can read well.

5. Avery ate an apple.

6. He is going to play baseball.

7. Mikel painted a picture.

8. Yoshi will take the test.

▶ **Revisit a piece of your writing. Edit the draft to make sure future-tense verbs are used correctly.**

Future Using *Will*

You can write sentences that tell about something that is going to happen. Use **will** to write sentences about the future.

▶ **Circle the sentences that tell about the future.**

1. I run each day.

2. My mom will help me skate.

3. Danny will clean his room.

4. She reads a letter.

▶ **Rewrite each sentence to tell about the future. Use the word will.**

5. Uma spelled her name.

_____

- - - - - - - - - - - - - - - - - - - -

_____

6. Brice collects action figures.

_____

- - - - - - - - - - - - - - - - - - - -

_____

7. We arrived late.

_____

- - - - - - - - - - - - - - - - - - - -

_____

Future Using *Going to*

You can write sentences that tell about something that will happen. Use **going to** to write sentences about the future.

▶ **Circle the sentences that tell about the future.**

1. They are going to skate.

3. Gina has a dog.

2. Kendrick has a pet lizard.

4. He is going to feed the fish.

▶ **Rewrite each sentence to tell about the future. Use the words *going to*.**

5. We planted flowers.

_____

_____

6. Mom played a game.

_____

_____

7. Julian fixes a snack.

_____

_____

▶ **Revisit a piece of your writing. Edit the draft to make sure future-tense verbs are used correctly.**

Review Future Tense

> Verbs can tell what is happening now, in the past, or in the future. Verbs with **will** or **going to** tell about the future.

▶ **Circle each sentence that tells about the future.**

1. Julie is going to write a book.

2. Doug fed the cat.

3. Kwame plays with his pet mouse.

4. She is going to play tennis.

5. We picked out a new bike.

6. My dad built a new shelf.

7. Ann and Jan are going to come over.

8. Iesha will dance in the show.

9. Miguel is going to set the table.

10. Her cousin rides horses.

▶ **Revisit a piece of your writing. Edit the draft to make sure future-tense verbs are used correctly.**

Connect to Writing: Using the Future Tense

▶ **Read the selection and choose the best answer to each question.**

> Gabi wrote a passage about learning to swim. Read her paragraph and look for any revisions she should make. Then answer the questions that follow.

(1) I want to learn how to swim. (2) The swimming lessons are fun. (3) I will practice a lot. (4) I will learn to float. (5) I am going to practice holding my breath under water. (6) I am going to learn proper arm strokes. (7) I enjoy learning to swim.

1. Which two sentences contain future-tense verbs?

   A. Sentences 1 and 2   B. Sentences 2 and 3

   C. Sentences 3 and 7   D. Sentences 4 and 5

2. Which sentence does NOT contain a future-tense verb?

   A. Sentence 2   B. Sentence 3

   C. Sentence 5   D. Sentence 6

▶ **What activity would you like to learn how to do? Write two or three sentences about your plans. Use will and going to to write about the future.**

Adjectives

> Some words describe people, animals, places, or things.
> These describing words are called **adjectives**. Adjectives
> can describe **size** or **shape**.
>
> The tree is <u>**tall**</u>. (size)   The plate is <u>**round**</u>. (shape)

▶ **Choose an adjective from the Word Bank to complete
each sentence. Write the adjective on the line.**

> round   tiny   square   large   curved

1. An ant is _____
_____.

2. A rainbow is _____
_____.

3. The baseball is _____
_____.

4. That _____ elephant weighs almost four tons!
_____

5. A checkerboard is _____
_____.

Adjectives for Size and Shape

> An **adjective** describes a noun. Adjectives can describe **size**. Adjectives can also describe **shape**.

▶ **Circle the adjective in ( ) that correctly completes each sentence. Write the adjective on the line.**

1. The big truck needs a _____ parking spot. (wide, small)

   _____

2. Roll out the clay to make it _____ (fast, flat)

   _____

3. Use the ruler's edge to draw a _____ line. (huge, straight)

   _____

4. The _____ tadpole will become a frog. (tiny, tall)

   _____

5. Sonia's _____ hair reaches past her shoulders.

   _____ (long, oval)

▶ **Revisit a piece of your writing. Edit the draft to make sure adjectives that describe size and shape are used correctly.**

Using Articles

The words **a**, **an**, and **the** are special adjectives called **articles**. **A** and **an** are used with nouns that name only one. **A** is used with nouns that begin with a consonant sound. **An** is used with nouns that begin with a vowel sound. The word **the** can be used with nouns that name one or more than one. **The** can be used with nouns that begin with a vowel sound or a consonant sound.

▶ **Circle the article that correctly completes each sentence. Then write it on the line.**

1. Janelle went to (a, an) party. _____

2. Nico peeled (a, an) orange. _____

3. David likes (an, the) the music. _____

4. We saw (a, an) eagle. _____

5. Linh found (the, an) coins. _____

Review Adjectives and Articles

Adjectives are words that describe people, animals, places, or things. Adjectives can describe **size** and **shape**.

▶ **Circle the adjective in each sentence. Then underline the noun it describes.**

1. Riku is holding the little puppy.

2. Shannon used a long ladder to reach the roof.

3. A plane landed at the huge airport.

▶ **Write the correct article (a, an, or the) that belongs in each sentence.**

4. We rode on _____ elevator.

5. What is _____ name of your school?

6. She thinks _____ flower is pretty.

7. Choose _____ pair of socks to wear.

Connect to Writing: Using Adjectives and Articles

▶ **Read the selection and choose the best answer to each question.**

> Kayla wrote a passage about her new kite. Read her paragraph and look for any revisions she should make. Then answer the questions that follow.

(1) I wanted a kite for my birthday. (2) My parents surprised me with it. (3) The kite was large and flat. (4) It was a triangle with a long tail. (5) The kite flew high when I ran with it. (6) My brother and I loved it. (7) It was a best gift ever.

1. Which two sentences have adjectives that describe the size and shape of the kite?

   A. Sentences 1 and 2   **B.** Sentences 4 and 5

   C. Sentences 3 and 4   **D.** Sentences 6 and 7

2. What change could Kayla make to improve sentence 7?

   A. Change a to an.   **B.** Change a to the.

   C. Change It to The.   **D.** Make no change.

▶ **What present would you like for your birthday? Write two or three sentences about it.**

Adjectives

Some words describe people, animals, places, or things. These describing words are called **adjectives**. Adjectives can describe color or number.

The house is <u>red</u>.   The <u>six</u> apples are <u>green</u>.

▶ **Circle the adjective that describes color or number in each sentence. Write the adjective on the line.**

1. Mary found five shells on the beach. _____

2. My mom grows pink roses. _____

3. Can we ride your brother's green bike? _____

4. We waited for two hours. _____

5. Jackson lost his blue backpack. _____

▶ **Revisit a piece of your writing. Edit the draft to make sure adjectives are used correctly.**

Adjectives for Color

> An **adjective** describes a noun. Adjectives can describe **color**.

▶ **Circle the adjective that describes color in each sentence. Then underline the noun it describes.**

1. She sat in the (flat, white) chair.

2. We are looking for a (three, gray) cat.

3. The grass is (pretty, green).

4. Dante got a new (fast, red) skateboard.

5. I want to smell that (huge, purple) flower.

▶ **Revisit a piece of your writing. Edit the draft to make sure adjectives that describe color are used correctly.**

Grade 1 • Adjectives: Color and Number
Printable
117

Adjectives for Number

> An **adjective** describes a noun. Adjectives can describe **number**.

▶ **Circle the adjective that describes number in each sentence. Then underline the noun it describes.**

1. We counted (bright, six) trucks.

2. Neila has (orange, three) new markers.

3. Maurice's cat had (five, small) kittens.

4. A car has (round, four) tires.

5. My house has (ten, big) windows.

▶ **Revisit a piece of your writing. Edit the draft to make sure adjectives that describe number are used correctly.**

Review Adjectives

Adjectives are words that describe people, animals, places, or things. Adjectives can describe a noun's color or tell how many.

▶ **Read each sentence. Circle the adjective for color.**

1. The bunny is (white, fluffy).

2. Stack the (red, hard) bricks in a pile.

3. Dante drives a (big, blue) car.

▶ **Read each sentence. Circle the adjective for number.**

4. I had (round, two) eggs for breakfast.

5. Ms. Shiraz asked us (short, five) questions.

6. Tom has visited (six, nice) countries.

▶ **Read each sentence. Underline the adjective. Circle if the adjective describes color or number.**

7. Please pass me the yellow pencil. (color, number)

8. Kwan chose two books at the library. (color, number)

9. My baby brother slept for eight hours. (color, number)

10. Aunt Celine lives in a red house. (color, number)

Connect to Writing: Using Adjectives for Color and Number

▶ Read the selection and choose the best answer to each question.

Pedro wrote a passage about cleaning his bedroom. Read his paragraph and look for any revisions he should make. Then answer the questions that follow.

(1) I cleaned my bedroom today. (2) I found so many things in there! (3) I found one red car. (4) I found six yellow blocks. (5) I found two green socks. (6) I could not find my blue marbles. (7) My room looks great now!

1. Which two sentences have adjectives that describe both color and number?

   A. Sentences 1 and 2   B. Sentences 2 and 4

   C. Sentences 3 and 6   D. Sentences 4 and 5

2. Which sentence has only one adjective, describing color?

   A. Sentence 3   B. Sentence 4

   C. Sentence 6   D. Sentence 7

▶ What are some colorful things you have at home? Write two or three sentences about them.

Adjectives

> Some **adjectives** describe nouns by telling about **taste**, **smell**, **sound**, or **feel**.
>
> spicy
> Example: I took a bite of the ∧ dish.

▶ Use the proofreading mark to add an adjective from the Word Bank to each sentence.

> fast   sweet   loud   warm   crunchy

Proofreading Marks	
∧	add

1. The duck made a quack.

2. Take the laundry out of the dryer.

3. We enjoy a dessert after dinner.

4. The car passed the truck.

5. Tara bit into the apple.

▶ Revisit a piece of your writing. Edit the draft to make sure adjectives for the senses are used correctly.

Adjectives for Taste and Smell

> Some **adjectives** describe nouns by telling how they **taste** or **smell**.

▶ **Draw a line under each adjective. Then write the adjective.**

1. There are sweet grapes in the fruit salad.

   _____

   - - - - - - - - - - - - - - - - -

   _____

2. Put your smelly socks in the washing machine.

   _____

   - - - - - - - - - - - - - - - - -

   _____

3. Did you taste the tart lemonade?   _____

   - - - - - - - - - - - - - - -

   _____

4. Mom made a tangy soup.   _____

   - - - - - - - - - - - - - - -

   _____

5. Dad's aftershave has a spicy fragrance.   _____

   - - - - - - - - - - - - - - -

   _____

▶ **Revisit a piece of your writing. Edit the draft to make sure adjectives for the senses are used correctly.**

Adjectives for Sound and Texture

Some **adjectives** describe nouns by telling how they **sound** or **feel**.

▶ **Draw a line under each adjective. Then write the adjective.**

1. We drove down the bumpy road. _____

2. He fell on the slippery ice. _____

3. I hear the loud waves crashing. _____

4. The booming thunder woke us up. _____

5. The yoga teacher plays soothing music. _____

▶ **Revisit a piece of your writing. Edit the draft to make sure adjectives for the senses are used correctly.**

Review Adjectives

Some **adjectives** describe by telling how things **taste**, **smell**, **sound**, or **feel**.

▶ **Circle the adjective in each sentence. Then underline the noun it describes.**

1. She baked a delicious cake.

2. They ate some sour candy.

3. My clock has a loud alarm.

4. He felt warm sand under his feet.

5. We ate some salty peanuts.

6. She had stinky feet.

7. I hid behind the rough rock.

8. The garden had a sweet scent.

9. I like to eat crunchy cereal.

10. The firecrackers made a popping noise.

▶ **Revisit a piece of your writing. Edit the draft to make sure adjectives for the senses are used correctly.**

Connect to Writing:
Using Adjectives for the Senses

▶ **Read the selection and choose the best answer to each question.**

> Gabe wrote a passage about his trip to a farm. Read his paragraph and look for any revisions he should make. Then answer the questions that follow.

(1) We took a trip to a farm. (2) The air smelled crisp and clean. (3) I scattered some gritty feed for the chickens. (4) They ate fast and made loud clucks. (5) I fed the piglets. (6) The piglets made noisy squeals. (7) We had fresh corn, and it tasted sweet.

1. Which two sentences contain adjectives that describe the smell, taste, sound, or feel of things at the farm?

   A. Sentence 1 and 4   **B.** Sentence 2 and 3

   C. Sentence 4 and 5   **D.** Sentence 5 and 6

2. Which sentence does NOT have adjectives that describe the smell, taste, sound, or feel of things at the farm?

   A. Sentence 1   **B.** Sentence 2

   C. Sentence 3   **D.** Sentence 4

Adjectives That Compare

> Add **-er** to adjectives to compare two. Add **-est** to compare more than two.
>
> My sister is **taller** than Colin.
>
> My sister is the **tallest** girl in the class.

▶ **Circle the adjective that makes a comparison.**

1. The red apple is sweeter than the green one.

2. Jose is the strongest of all six cousins.

3. July was the hottest month this year.

4. My little brother talks faster than I do.

5. Wear your older sneakers to play outside.

▶ **Revisit a piece of your writing. Edit the draft to make sure adjectives that compare are used correctly.**

Adjectives with -er and -est

> Add **-er** to adjectives to compare two. Add **-est** to adjectives to compare more than two.

▶ **Circle the correct adjective in ( ) to finish each sentence. Write the adjective on the line.**

1. Patrick is _____ than Tony. (younger   youngest)

2. Maria is the _____ student in her class.
   (older   oldest)

3. James is _____ than Witt. (taller   tallest)

4. Paola is the _____ runner on the team.
   (faster   fastest)

5. The basement is the _____ place in the house.
   (darker   darkest)

▶ **Revisit a piece of your writing. Edit the draft to make sure adjectives that compare are used correctly.**

Using the Right Adjective

Add **-er** to adjectives to compare two. Add **-est** to
adjectives to compare more than two.

▶ **Write an adjective from the Word Bank to finish
each sentence.**

| firmer | loudest | longer | sharpest | sweeter |

1. This melon is _____ than the cherries.

2. Amelia's hair is _____ than her sister's.

3. Kyle has the _____ laugh of anyone.

4. The couch cushions are _____ than my
pillow.

5. Mom took out the _____ knife in the drawer.

▶ **Revisit a piece of your writing. Edit the draft to make
sure adjectives that compare are used correctly.**

Review Adjectives That Compare

Add **-er** to adjectives to compare two. Add **-est** to adjectives to compare more than two.

▶ **Circle an adjective in ( ) to take the place of the blank in each sentence.**

1. This movie is _____. (long, longest)

2. This movie is the _____ one I've seen. (longer, longest)

3. This movie is _____ that the last one. (longer, longest)

4. My parents' room is the _____ of all. (cleaner, cleanest)

5. My brother's room is _____ than mine. (clean, cleaner)

6. I have a _____ room. (clean, cleanest)

7. We ate at the _____ restaurant in town. (newer, newest)

8. My friends own the _____ restaurant. (new, newer)

9. Today was the _____ day of the year. (colder, coldest)

10. Yesterday was _____ than the day before.
   (colder, coldest)

▶ **Revisit a piece of your writing. Edit the draft to make sure adjectives that compare are used correctly.**

Connect to Writing:
Using Adjectives That Compare

▶ **Read the selection and choose the best answer to each question.**

> Jessica wrote a passage about her track team. Read her paragraph and look for any revisions she should make. Then answer the questions that follow.

(1) We have a strong track team. (2) Marion is a fastest runner. (3) I am even faster than she is. (4) Florence is the fastest runner on the team. (5) We have excellent jumpers. (6) Darren jumps over the high bar. (7) Jesse jumps over the high bar of all.

1. What change, if any, should be made to sentence 2?

   A. Change fastest to faster. **B.** Change fastest to fast.

   C. Change Marion to she. **D.** Make no change.

2. What change, if any, should be made to sentence 7?

   A. Change high to higher. **B.** Change high to highs.

   C. Change high to highest. **D.** Make no change.

▶ **What activity have you done with others? Write two or three sentences about it.**

Grade 1 • Adjectives That Compare

Adverbs

> An **adverb** is a word that describes a verb.
> Adverbs can tell **how**, **where**, **when**, or **how much**. Many, but not all, adverbs end in **-ly**.
>
> She walked <u>**quickly**</u> across the room.
> **How** did she walk? quickly

▶ **Circle the adverb in each sentence.**

1. She gently patted the kitten.

2. He found the book there.

3. My mom smiled cheerfully.

4. We will eat our pizza later.

5. We watched the bee closely.

▶ **Revisit a piece of your writing. Edit the draft to make sure adverbs are used correctly.**

Adverbs for How and Where

An **adverb** is a word that describes a verb. Adverbs can tell **how** an action was done or **where** an action happened.

Otis sleeps **deeply**.
How does Otis sleep? deeply

I see flowers **everywhere**.
Where do I see flowers? everywhere

▶ **Circle the adverb in each sentence.**

1. Carissa wisely put her money in the bank.

2. Ben went upstairs.

3. We found the box here.

4. Nina carefully made her bed.

5. Dad drives his car slowly into the garage.

▶ **Revisit a piece of your writing. Edit the draft to make sure adverbs are used correctly.**

Adverbs for When and How Much

An **adverb** is a word that describes a verb. Adverbs can tell **when** and **how much**.

We will go to the movies **tomorrow**.
When will we go? tomorrow

Lydia **almost** finished her dinner.
How much did Lydia finish? almost

▶ **Circle the adverb in each sentence.**

1. We will have pizza soon.

2. We ordered enough pizza.

3. Dan arrived late to the movie.

4. Roni completely missed the waste basket.

5. My dog was very happy to see me.

▶ **Revisit a piece of your writing. Edit the draft to make sure all adverbs are used correctly.**

Review Adverbs

Adverbs are words that describe verbs. An adverb can tell **how**, **where**, **when**, and **how much**. Many, but not all, adverbs end in **-ly**.

They **carefully** steered the boat.
How did they steer? carefully
They're **here**!   **Where** are they? here

▶ **Circle the adverb in each sentence. Then write if it tells how, where, when, or how much.**

1. The car moves quickly. _____
   _____
   _____

2. They woke up late. _____
   _____
   _____

3. The milk spilled everywhere. _____
   _____
   _____

4. The play is nearly finished. _____
   _____
   _____

5. My friend waved happily to me. _____
   _____
   _____

Connect to Writing:
Using Adverbs

▶ **Read the selection and choose the best answer to each question.**

> Meg wrote the following paragraph about a trip to the zoo. Read her paragraph and look for any revisions she should make. Then answer the questions that follow.

(1) My family and I like to visit the zoo. (2) We always go to the bird exhibits. (3) We buy seed sticks and quietly enter the birds' home. (4) They fly around us. (5) Then they peck at the seeds. (6) I think they are thanking us for feeding them.

1. Which example shows how Meg could rewrite sentence 1 to include an adverb?

   A. My family and I like to visit the big zoo.

   B. My family and I like to visit the zoo often.

2. Adverbs can make writing more specific and interesting. Which sentence below could replace sentence 4 to make it more interesting?

   A. They fly around us eagerly. **B.** They fly above us.

Name _____

Prepositions and Prepositional Phrases

A **preposition** tells **where** something is or **when** something happens. A **prepositional phrase** is a group of words that begins with a preposition.

The banana is **on the table**.
Where is the banana?
Preposition: on   Prepositional phrase: on the table

▶ **Circle the prepositional phrase in each sentence. Write the preposition on the line.**

1. The nest is in the tree. _____

2. The birds sing before sunrise. _____

3. The cat hid under the chair. _____

4. The dog jumped over the fence. _____

5. We play games after dinner _____

Prepositions for Where

> A **preposition** and **prepositional phrase** can tell where something is located.
>
> The school is <u>**down the street**</u>.
>
> **Where** is the school?
>
> Preposition: down   Prepositional phrase: down the street

▶ **Circle the prepositional phrase in each sentence.**

1. Rachel went to Clara's house.

2. She walked up the steps.

3. She knocked on the door.

▶ **Complete each sentence. Write a prepositional phrase that tells where.**

4. A bear sleeps _____

_____.

5. The goat climbs _____

_____.

▶ **Revisit a piece of your writing. Edit the draft to make sure prepositions and prepositional phrases are used correctly.**

Grade 1 • Prepositions and Prepositional Phrases

Prepositions for When

A **preposition** and **prepositional phrase** can tell when something happens.

We made masks **during art class**.

When did we make masks?

Preposition: during   Prepositional phrase: during art class

▶ **Circle the prepositional phrase in each sentence.**

1. We wash the dishes after lunch.

2. Dad comes home at 5 o'clock.

3. We leave the park before dark.

4. During recess, we play soccer.

5. I will read until I am done.

▶ **Revisit a piece of your writing. Edit the draft to make sure prepositions and prepositional phrases are used correctly.**

Review Prepositions and Prepositional Phrases

A **preposition** joins with other words to explain where something is or when it happens. A **prepositional phrase** is a group of words that starts with a preposition.

The dog sleeps <u>under a tree</u>.

The dog sleeps <u>after he eats</u>.

▶ Circle the prepositional phrase in each sentence. Decide if the prepositional phrase tells where or when. Write where or when on the line.

1. Suki read a book before dinner. _____

2. We eat dinner at 6 o'clock. _____

3. The cat creeps across the grass. _____

4. She raced through the trees. _____

5. I hear something above my head. _____

Connect to Writing: Using Prepositions and Prepositional Phrases

▶ **Read the selection and choose the best answer to each question.**

> Dhani wrote the following paragraph about his birthday. Read his paragraph and look for any revisions he should make. Then answer the questions that follow.

(1) My last birthday party was at the park. (2) We played hide-and-seek, and I hid behind a tree. (3) We hung a piñata. (4) Dad served us cake. (5) Before I blew out the candles, I made a wish.

1. How could Dhani change sentence 3 to include a prepositional phrase?

   A. We hung a piñata on a tree branch.

   B. We hung a piñata and some balloons.

2. How could Dhani change sentence 4 to include a prepositional phrase?

   A. After we broke the piñata, Dad served us cake.

   B. Dad finally served us cake and ice cream.

Contractions

> A **contraction** is a short way of writing two words. Two words become one and this mark (') takes the place of missing letters. It is called an **apostrophe**.
>
> it's = it is   don't = do not
>
> she's = she is   I'm = I am

▶ **Circle the contraction in each sentence. Write the two words that the contraction stands for.**

1. He's going to the store. _____

_____

2. I'm very hungry. _____

_____

3. I don't have practice today. _____

_____

4. Aki isn't home now. _____

_____

5. They're washing windows. _____

_____

Grade 1 • Contractions

Printable
141

Contractions with Not

A **contraction** is a short way of writing two words or a long word. Many contractions include the word not.

do not = don't   is not = isn't   cannot = can't

▶ **Write the contraction for the underlined word or words. Use contractions from the Word Bank. You may use words more than once.**

isn't   aren't   can't   don't

1. He <u>is not</u> at school. _____

2. I <u>do not</u> know where my books are. _____

3. They <u>are not</u> on the shelf. _____

4. I <u>cannot</u> find my pencil. _____

5. I <u>do not</u> have an eraser. _____

Contractions with Pronouns

A **contraction** is a short way of writing two words as one. Many contractions include pronouns.

I'm = I am   he's = he is   we're = we are

▶ **Write the contraction for the underlined words. Use contractions from the Word Bank. You may use words more than once.**

I'm   it's   she's   they're

1. <u>It is</u> time for the movie to start. _____

2. Chaya said <u>she is</u> ready. _____

3. <u>They are</u> planning a party. _____

4. <u>I am</u> going to help the teacher. _____

5. I think <u>it is</u> going to rain. _____

Review Contractions

> A **contraction** is a short way of writing two words or a long word. An **apostrophe** (') takes the place of missing letters.

▶ **Write the contraction for the underlined word or words in each sentence.**

1. Next week <u>I am</u> going to the dentist. _____

2. My cousins said <u>they are</u> moving. _____

3. Jacob <u>is not</u> finished eating. _____

4. <u>We are</u> waiting in line. _____

5. I hope <u>she is</u> coming to visit. _____

Connect to Writing: Using Contractions

▶ **Read the selection and choose the best answer to each question.**

> Alonso wrote the following paragraph about adopting a pet. Read his paragraph and look for any revisions he should make. Then answer the questions that follow.

(1) My family wants to adopt a puppy. (2) W'ere planning on going to the shelter to rescue a puppy. (3) My dad wants a husky. (4) My mom wants a pug. (5) They are cute and small. (6) It doesn't matter to me if our puppy is a husky or a pug.

1. What change to sentence 2 would make the sentence correct?

  A. Change W'ere to Wer'e.   **B.** Change W'ere to We'are.

  C. Change W'ere to We're.   **D.** Make no change.

2. What change could Alonso make to sentence 5?

  A. Change They are to They're.

  B. Change They are to They were.

  C. Change They are to The'yre.

  D. There is no change to make.

Spelling Words with Short and Long Vowels

Words can have short vowel sounds. These words sometimes have a consonant-vowel-consonant, or **CVC**, pattern. Words can have long vowel sounds. These words sometimes have a consonant-vowel-consonant-e, or **CVCe**, pattern. The vowels in these words say their own name.

Short Vowel Words with CVC		Long Vowel Words with Silent e	
lap	top	lake	bone
pet	pup	eve	cube
sit		kite	

▶ **Circle the word that is spelled correctly in each sentence.**

1. The barber put a (cap, cape) around Fred.

2. The hair dryer blew a (fus, fuse).

3. The barber swept the (rug, ruge).

4. Fred asked to (get, gete) ice cream.

5. Fred and his dad ate an ice cream (con, cone).

Spelling Words with Endings

Some words need an ending. For example, you might add -s or -es to a verb to make it match its subject. You add -s or -es to a noun to show more than one.
Adding -ed or -ing changes a verb.

Add -s or -es	Add -ed or -ing
Bill gets a new hat.	Bill added some mittens, too.
The hat matches his coat.	He is going to be warm!

▶ **Circle the word in ( ) that correctly completes the sentence.**

1. Jason (gos, goes) shopping.

2. His mom (buyes, buys) some new clothes.

3. Jason (puts, putes) his new things away.

4. Emily (followed, followeed) her mom into the store.

5. She is (tryeing, trying) on a new outfit.

▶ **Revisit a piece of your writing. Edit the draft to make sure all words are spelled correctly.**

Spelling High-Frequency Words

Some words are used often in writing. It is important to learn to spell them correctly.

Common Words		Question Words	
after	know	who	where
every	open	what	why
going	some	when	how

▶ **Circle the word that is spelled correctly in each sentence.**

1. Marcus (might, mite) get a new bike.

2. Marcus (culd, could) pick a blue bike.

3. It will come (from, frum) the store.

4. Marcus (livs, lives) near the store.

5. Many (peeple, people) buy bikes there.

▶ **Revisit a piece of your writing. Edit the draft to make sure all words are spelled correctly.**

Review Spelling

Some words can be misspelled easily. Check to be sure you spell words correctly.

Short Vowel Words: bed, pin, pan

Long Vowel Words: stone, date

High-Frequency Words: what, some, know

▶ **Circle the word that is spelled correctly in each sentence.**

1. Roxy wanted a new (pet, pete).

2. Her mom (tolked, talked) about a dog.

3. They went to the (shellter, shelter).

4. They were not sure (howe, how) to choose.

5. The puppies (barkeed, barked).

6. (Sum, Some) licked her fingers.

7. They saw a (cut, cute), brown pup.

8. They (asked, aksed) to adopt her.

9. Roxy and her mom took the puppy (homm, home).

10. Roxy will (walk, wolk) the pup each day.

▶ **Revisit a piece of your writing. Edit the draft to make sure all words are spelled correctly.**

Connect to Writing: Using Correct Spelling

▶ **Read the selection and choose the best answer to each question.**

> Maya wrote the following paragraph about raking leaves. Read her story and look for any revisions she should make. Then answer the questions that follow.

(1) I lick to rake leaves. (2) They make a quiet, rustling sound. (3) I make big piles of leaves. (4) My brother runs and jumps into the piles. (5) He pushs all the leaves away. (6) Then, I rake them up again. (7) Mom brings us hot chocolate. (8) We warm up, then we start over!

1. Which of the following should replace the word lick in sentence 1 so that it is spelled correctly?

   A. lik   **B.** like

   C. lice   **D.** licke

2. What change, if any, should be made to sentence 5?

   A. Change pushs to pushes.   **B.** Change leaves to leafs.

   C. Change away to alway.   **D.** Make no change.
